Decluttering Your Home

The Fast Way to Get Rid of Clutter and Organize Your Life

By Priscilla Pritchard

First Edition, March 2012

INTRODUCTION

At some point, you might have looked around your home or your office and thought to yourself: there has to be a better way.

After looking for your keys for the hundredth time, and having to spend an hour just trying to get out the door, you wished things could be different. Even if you are an organized person, sometimes, you realize that all of the systems you have in place don't always work as well as they could.

Or perhaps you're someone who doesn't have any systems in place, or you've held onto certain items for a while, even though you don't know why you 'need' them around. Still, you amass new things, adding to piles in your bedroom, in your closets, and beneath your beds.

The more you begin to see the clutter in your life, the more powerless you can feel to control it. While you know you need to get rid of things, you also know that it's easier said than done. You've started to organize by throwing things away, only to begin to collect more things.

What are you supposed to do?

Perhaps it's not as simple as getting rid of excess items. Perhaps it's not as simple as labeling drawers and putting things in certain places.

In this book, you will learn about how you can get your life under control, because that's the underlying problem for most of us. When we feel out of control, our environment shows it. And when we can declutter our life and organize our possessions, we can begin to live in a new way.

Imagine what your life will be like when you know where to find your keys, when you have a closet filled with items you actually use, and when you have a sense of where everything is all of the time.

Impossible? Not at all. What you need right now is a gentle push in the right direction.

WHAT CAUSES CLUTTER?

The simple explanation for the clutter in your home might appear to be that you own too many things. While this is certainly true, it's not the whole story.

Without going into an extensive therapy program, your clutter is about more than what you own – it's about WHY you own it.

Though you might not realize it, you're holding onto the items you have, not because you want things to be chaotic, but because you need these items for other reasons – and not all of these reasons are practical.

When you can begin to understand why you have the things you do, you can start to change the way that you take new items into your life. You'll give it a bit more thought when you're in a store and you see something you have to have.

And over time, you will begin to own less, but value what you have more.

WORRY ABOUT NOT HAVING ENOUGH

Even if you've never been in a position of not having enough, you might still have this worry. With all of the news about an inconsistent

3

economy, you look around at the possessions you have and you wonder if you have enough.

So when you're out a store, you might look at the deals on certain essentials, for example. Since you might be worried that you may not have the money in the future, you buy up all that you can and then you store it in your home.

In a certain sense, this is actually a very reasonable way to approach shopping. You need something, you buy it. But when you worry constantly about not having enough in your life, you may begin to amass larger quantities of things than you actually DO need.

Think about the bulk stores and how they offer hundred-roll packs of toilet paper. While eventually you might need it, right now, you will simply just store it in your house, taking up space and creating clutter where you don't want to have clutter.

A person who is worried about not having enough:

- Might be stressed out about money.

- Might have felt in the past that they didn't have what they needed.

- Might be afraid that if they don't buy something now, they might not be able to have it in the future.

These worries are valid, but they also may be causing you to have items in your home that you don't need/don't have the space to store.

SENTIMENTAL ATTACHMENT

Many others will find they hold onto items that are sentimental to them. This might include everything from gifts from others to photographs, cards, and more.

They associate the item with the feeling they have about the person from whom they received it, or they might feel that giving away the item means they don't care about the other person.

You might have boxes of these sentimental items in your home, or they might be sitting out on tables and shelves, taking up space and creating a cluttered look.

When this is the case, you end up having these items in your life, but they also might be blocking you from having space for new sentimental items.

WORRY ABOUT WASTING MONEY

In today's economy, many people don't like to throw things away, especially when they've paid good money for them. You feel that if you get rid of an item, you're also throwing away the money that you spent on it.

And if you throw away the item, you're not only giving up that initial investment, but you also might have to re-buy the item in the future, which means you're going to spend twice as much for one item.

This makes perfect sense when you're worried about your financial situation.

WANTING TO HAVE LOTS OF THE BEST THINGS

Others may buy a number of items because they want to have a lot of the best things in their lives. What this means is that when you buy something that you really enjoy, you might buy more than one item in order to ensure you always have this item in your life.

This is often seen in those who have a lot of technology items, as they want to have a lot of these items – even if you can't use them all at the same time.

Again, this can become a costly venture, and it can also create a sort of scattered approach to your organization, since you begin to forget what each item provides you in terms of value.

So you buy something else.

DEPRESSION

If you've been feeling down in your life, you want to get rid of that feeling as quickly as possible. For many people, the 'cure' might be to buy something new that will give you a burst of excitement.

And buying things does work for some people.

But the trick with depression-influenced buying is that it's a vicious cycle. You buy something that will make you feel better, and it works for a while. Then the excitement of the item goes away and you end up feeling down and depressed again.

So you buy something else...and then you start ending up with more clutter, which can also cause you feel more depressed about your life.

DENIAL

Some people will have more clutter in their lives because they don't admit that they have clutter in the first place. You know someone like this, and it might even include yourself.

This is a person who buys more items and more items, only to run out of room. Then they might start storing the items in a storage facility or in an unused closet, hidden from sight.

They continue to buy more because they deny the idea that they already have enough – but you can see where this can become problematic if you also want to organize your life.

If you deny that there is an issue with clutter, the clutter is going to take over more quickly than you may anticipate (or desire).

GRIEF

Like depression, grief can be tricky when you're trying to handle your clutter. Whether you've lost a loved one or you have lost a job or a partnership, you might begin to feel sad.

This sadness can be temporarily relieved by buying something and by bringing something new into your life. Or you might be tempted to hold onto everything you already have, as you don't want to lose anything else.

However, grief then becomes a collection of items to surround you, rather than an opportunity for you to feel sad and eventually feel better as time goes on.

BEING RAISED BY PEOPLE WITH CLUTTER

While your parents may never admit it, often there are issues with clutter that can begin with how you were raised. If you're surrounded by clutter all the time, or people who don't believe clutter is an issue surround you, you can feel the same way.

It doesn't seem strange, and it certainly doesn't seem to be a problem.

No matter what your reason for hanging onto clutter, you can take action right now to change the way that your life looks and how it is organized. You can take control back – and you can let go of the clutter that may be hindering you from feeling truly happy.

REMEMBER THAT YOU ARE NOT YOUR STUFF

In today's society, the mantra seems to be 'more is more' instead of 'less is more.' We think that the more we have, the better we are – or the more successful we are.

But if you've picked up this book, you've already begun to suspect this isn't the truth.

Instead of hanging onto the life that you have right now, let's think about what might happen if you were to get rid of the clutter in your life – for good. Even though it might not seem that clutter is holding you back too much, the following benefits may just change your mindset.

LESS STUFF CAN MEAN LESS STRESS

When you own 1000 books, you need to keep track of these books. You need to move them when you have to move, you need to look through all of them when you want to choose something to read, etc.

More stuff = more stress

If you begin to remove things from your life, you don't have to experience this stress, as you can focus on other things in your life, besides what you own.

With a decluttered and organized life, you will:

- Be able to find what you need.

- Be able to know what you need to buy and what you don't.

- No longer buy duplicate items because you can't remember what you own.

- Spend less money.

- Focus on activities instead of possessions (think trips vs. souvenirs).

When you own less, you will no long be owned by the things you have in your home.

Instead, you can focus on what you already have and enjoy those items, which is a much more freeing experience than you may realize right now.

PLACE LIMITS ON HOW MUCH STUFF YOU HAVE

But the truth is that you will have to buy things in order to help maintain your life and the activities you need to do in order to live. So, a good first step is to think about the idea that you are not your stuff. Your stuff is just a series of things that you own, but you are a separate person, someone with value, even if you owned nothing.

To start changing the way you think about possessions, as this is a new experience for many, you need to start limiting the items you bring into your home.

You need to start thinking about what you want to have and what you want to get rid of, as well.

How can you place limits on what you have in your home?

- Promise not to bring anything else in. If you don't need to buy something, don't buy it.

- Exchange two items for every one item you buy. What this means is that each time you buy something new, you need to remove two items from your home to ensure you have enough space.

- Have a no-buying ban. Many people today are going on spending diets to help them control their clutter. For example, you might spend a month or two not buying anything that isn't essential. Just in trying out this practice, you will find that you can go for longer periods of time, and be reducing your clutter without having to get rid of anything.

Some find that limiting the items they have sitting on tables or on shelves can help to create better control over their clutter.

For example, you might have a rule that the shelves in your home can only hold as many books as there are shelves. No books can be stacked on top of other books or on the top of the shelf.

If there are extra books in those areas, they need to find a new home or they need to be given away.

Other ways to place limits on the clutter in your home include:

- Keeping counters free of clutter.

- Keeping tables free of clutter.

This might look like a practice of every night removing items that are on these surfaces, putting the items away. In time, you might find that you no longer place items in these areas, which will allow you to slowly transition to a clutter-free home.

WHERE TO START

You may already know how to declutter, how to throw things away, and how to get organized. But the truth is that you don't know where to start, and that can derail even the best plans.

You need a bit of help to get things started, but once you're on a roll, you'll be decluttering and organizing everything you can see.

HOW TO GET THE MOTIVATION TO DECLUTTER

Maybe you need some motivation to get started, maybe not. To get things started, it can help for you to list all of the reasons why should get rid of the extra items in your home:

- More money

- More space

- Less stress

- More organization

These are the four biggest reasons to declutter, but since you probably already know these reasons personally, it might help for you to go to someone else's house, someone who keeps their space clutter free.

Or head to a hotel for a night or two. Look around at what it's like to not have things scattered around you. Enjoy the peace that comes with knowing exactly where your belongings are and being able to look around and not see messes.

Sometimes, that's the best motivation of all – feeling what it will be like when you finally reach your goal of getting organized and clutter-free.

You might also want to team up with someone else in your life who is facing clutter challenges. Make a pact with each other to work on your home's organization, and then check in on each other to make sure you're sticking to your plans.

And just like with weight loss, it can help to take a picture of the 'Before' in your home and then take 'After' pictures as you begin to declutter. The remarkable difference will spurn you on to continue your efforts.

HOW TO LET GO OF CLUTTER

Be honest with yourself right now – you already know how to declutter, but it's not as easy as knowing the steps. You also need to be able to let go of the things you no longer need in your life, so you can make room for new things.

16

Or so that you can just make room for yourself.

To let go of clutter, it can help to embrace a three-step system. This will help you clearly think about each thing that you are considering getting rid of, and it will allow you to feel in control of the process.

If you just start throwing things away, you might end up panicking, which can lead to a late-night shopping trip to get more things to put in the space you just freed up.

- Keep – First, you will want to look around your home and see what you want to keep. You can designate the keepers with small colored sticky notes, attaching them to the items you will hold onto as you organize.

- Donate – Think about things that are still useful, but that you no longer use. Those can be donated to local charities and thrift stores. Or you might want to donate them to friends and family if you feel they might want these items. Some of the larger charities will even come out to your home to pick up bigger items, so if you have furniture or appliances, you may want to check to see how these services can help make the donation process easier.

- Toss – And then there are the items that don't work, are in ill repair, etc. Get rid of things that are not going to give you any use anymore, and that no one else can use either.

The process starts with one room at a time. You will want to look around, see what you own, and then look to see how you can organize the room into three piles – keep, donate, and toss.

Start slowly and work your way around the room until everything (well, everything that can be moved) is in a pile. Once you've created the piles, then toss the items that need to be tossed in the trash bin or in a recycling bin.

Take the donation items to the thrift store or other charity.

All you'll have left are the items that you truly want to keep. And at this point, you can go through those items again to make sure there aren't any items that might still need to be donated or tossed.

The key is to remove the items from the room as quickly as possible so that you don't start rethinking all of your decisions. Go with your first instinct and then move onto something else.

You will find that when you don't give things a lot of thought, you can not only get rid of more, but you will also begin to see that you didn't really care about most of the items in the first place.

HOW TO DEAL WITH THE ANXIETY AND GUILT

Some people who have issues with clutter will begin to feel anxious when they start to get rid of things they own. They start to believe that they are wasting money or that they are hurting someone they love, especially if the person bought a certain item for them.

Here are some ways that you can deal with these very normal thoughts.

- Take pictures of sentimental items – When you have items that hold sentimental value to you, but you realize are just clutter now, think about taking a picture of them so that you can remember the item, but you don't have to hold onto the actual item. Store the picture in your computer to look at when you remember the item or the person who gave you the item.

- Remind yourself that you can replace the item – Each time you get rid of something in your life, remind yourself that 99% of the time you will be able to replace it again, even if you have to spend more money.

- Remind yourself of the benefits of decluttering – As you begin to remove items from your home, remind yourself of

19

the benefits you are also gaining: more space, more money, and less stress.

- Think about how much you have used the item – If you feel guilty about getting rid of something, look at the item and think about how many times you have used it. If you can't think of many times, then remind yourself that this item isn't bringing value to your life. And if something isn't bringing value to your life, then you need to get rid of it so that you have room to add things to your life that DO have value.

- See if you can give the item to someone else – Sometimes, when you feel guilty or anxious, it can help to give this item to someone else that you know. In doing so, you will know the item is going to be safe after you remove it from your life.

Some people might want to consider selling items they are no longer going to use, but that still work. Holding a garage sale or going to auction sites online can help you unload some of your possessions, and make a small amount of money.

The anxiety and the guilt is a very normal part of getting rid of items you've had for a while. But remember that you are not your things. Just because you own things doesn't make you a better person.

In fact, much of the time, having too many things will actually hold you back and prevent you from moving forward in your life.

HOW TO CONVINCE A HOARDER TO DECLUTTER

You've probably seen the TV shows where hoarders are told they need to clean out their homes or else.

But while those shows might be able to offer professional help, what about when you have someone in your life who is a hoarder? Can you help them to declutter their home?

Much of the time, you will hear a series of excuses from hoarders:

- It's not a problem.

- I'm taking care of it.

- It's not your house.

Though these excuses might seem reasonable to them, when hoarding gets out of hand, it can cause health problems, safety issues, and even legal issues in some areas.

To convince someone who is a hoarder to declutter, it might help to be a part of the process – at first, anyway. Offer to help them go through the things they have in order to get rid of items that might be unsanitary or unnecessary.

While it's true that this might be a difficult battle, letting the person know that you are available to help can often get the process started. At the same time, you need to encourage the person to see out help on their own – and often they need therapeutic support from a clinician too.

Hoarding can be caused by trauma in one's life, as well as by things like depression, OCD, and compulsive shopping. You can talk to your loved one about their issue, but you may not be the one to help them solve it completely.

Express to them your concerns about their safety and offer to get them the help they need – without bringing them onto a TV show.

KNOWING WHEN TO GET PROFESSIONAL HELP

Even if you or someone you know is not a hoarder, it can still be challenging to declutter and to organize a home. At times, it can seem as though getting professional help might be the best way to ensure you have the results you want. But when is it time to call in the professionals to help?

- When there are safety issues.

- When you have a hoarding situation.

- When the clutter has been present for many years.

- When you cannot complete the work on your own.

Professional help doesn't have to be a part of the entire process of your organization either. You might choose to handle the decluttering part, but then call in an organizer to help you get finished with everything.

Or you can have someone help you with the decluttering and then do the organizational work on your own.

Just realize that when you've already tried to get organized and decluttered a few times, and you just can't seem to finish the task on your own, you may want to call in someone who will be excited to help you.

HOW LONG WILL IT TAKE TO DECLUTTER?

Some people give up on decluttering before they even begin because they're concerned it will take a long time and they don't want to spend all of the time and the energy.

But decluttering can be a longer process for some people, though not for everyone. The length of your decluttering and organization process is impacted by the following situations:

- How much clutter you have

- How much help you have

- How large your space is

- How many resources you have – i.e. professional organizers

- How much of the clutter is psychologically based

- How much time you have available

And these are just the beginning of a longer list of things that can slow down the decluttering process.

The truth is that the decluttering process will take as long as it takes to be completed. Some can take months, others weeks, and others may take years to tackle all of their clutter.

This is not a process to rush, as you want to make sure that the next time you declutter and organize is also the LAST time you have to declutter and organize.

DECIDE WHAT TO KEEP, DONATE/RECYCLE, AND TRASH

We've already talked about the idea of having a keep, donate, and trash pile when you're starting the decluttering process. But while this makes sense, how can you choose what goes into each pile?

Instead of simply guessing, you might want to look at the items you have and see if there are ways to handle them so that you not only get rid of what you don't need, but that you also can get rid of things without immediately wanting them back in your home.

WHAT TO DO WITH...GIFTS

Gifts are often the trickiest situation when you have clutter. After all, you received these items from other people, so they weren't put into your home by you necessarily.

As a result, you might feel as though you have an obligation to hold onto these items, as though the other person will find out that you have not used them or enjoyed them.

In many cases, the person who buys you something will not even remember what they bought you in a few months, so you may want to release that idea from your brain. Instead, you need to look at the gifts you've received and ask yourself three questions:

- Do I like it?

- Will I use it?

- Have I used it?

Think about the true value the item will hold for you right now. If it doesn't seem to be adding to your joy in life, then it's time to get rid of it.

But you don't have to throw it away in order to remove this as clutter from your life. Instead, you can:

- Exchange it – If it hasn't been long since you received the item, you might want to go back to the store and see if you can get a store credit or exchange it for an item you will use.

- Sell it – You can also go onto online boards and try to sell the item to someone else so you can have cash instead of something you don't need or want.

- Re-gift it – If you have another friend with a special occasion coming up, then you can always send this gift to that friend, assuming the two will never meet. Or hold

a re-gifting party with other friends to exchange items that you may not want, but also to take in items from others that might be more valuable.

- Donate it – And if no one wants it and you can't sell it, try to donate it to an organization that will find value in what you have.

If you're still feeling guilty about getting rid of something that Aunt Madge gave you, take a picture of yourself with the item and hold onto that. This will allow you to have proof that you received it and you can always pull that picture out when your aunt comes to visit.

DOCUMENTS, RECEIPTS, AND TAX PAPERS

When you look around at the clutter that's in your drawers, office, and other business-related areas of your home, you might see more paper than other items.

All of that paperwork looks important, so you hang onto it, hoping that you will never need to find it. In most cases, you will rarely have to hold onto the paperwork that you receive.

Here are some things to keep in mind:

- If you can find it online again, throw away the paper copy.

- Only keep the original paper copy if it can't be replaced.

Those are two basic rules when it comes to paperwork. But let's work through each of the different types of paperwork you might have in your house right now.

DOCUMENTS

This can include everything from letters you've received to bills and other papers that you handle in an average week. Documents are tricky to declutter and to organize because you never know when you might need them.

If you're concerned about documents that you might need, you can always purchase or use a scanner to help you scan the information from the documents onto a computer, CD-ROM, or flash drive. This will take up far less space in your home, while still giving you access to your information, if needed.

Or you might want to simply shred and get rid of anything you can find again – i.e. billing statements. If you can reproduce the item in other ways, then remove it from your stacks of papers.

RECEIPTS

If you have to collect receipts for tax purposes, it can help to have a clearly defined area in which these are kept. Just like your other paperwork, you can also scan these receipts into your computer so you don't have to keep the paper copies.

Or you can invest in a filing folder into which you can place the receipts according to their purpose – i.e. entertainment, supplies, expenses, etc.

If you can't read a receipt, you will need to find a replacement for it, or you can just toss it to reduce your clutter.

Talk with your tax advisor about what receipts you might need to collect during the year, as this advice can also help you reduce clutter, especially when you aren't collecting every single receipt you pick up during a typical day.

TAX DOCUMENTS

While some experts recommend that you keep your tax documents for seven years, it's actually a better idea to keep them for 10 years, since this will help to ensure you have the right papers, should the IRS need to audit you or they just want to ask you a few questions about your tax return.

If you're not sure what to keep for your tax documents, here's a simple system that will help you collect it all into categories. When you have things organized, at least you will know where certain papers should be.

- House stuff

- Receipts

- Home business paperwork

- Income statements

- W-4s, 1099s

- Investment statements

- Interest statements

Think about the things that you generally have to claim or deduct from your taxes. Create a folder for each of those categories and you'll have a great system for filing your tax documents.

If you're not sure if you should get rid of something, you can also talk to the IRS to see what they recommend. Often, you can get rid of something that you can access in another way, i.e. online. But it never hurts to hold onto these types of papers for as long as you have room for them in your home – without creating clutter.

BABY ITEMS

Once you've had a child, you tend to buy a lot of items that will help them feel loved and supported as they grow up. But what happens to these items when your child has finally grown up – or even just grown out of the items?

That's where clutter can begin to increase. Though you might be interested in keeping those baby items around...just in case...you might want to rethink this strategy.

While it might be easier for you to keep the items around, you may also want to consider the space that your child needs as they are growing up. You need to make room for all of the big boy/girl things they need to keep in their room or their closet.

To make things easier, here are the baby items you definitely need to remove from your child's life:

- Baby bottles

- Baby onesies

- Chewing toys

- Ripped or ruined books

Look for things that you can replace cheaply or things that your child has already destroyed. This will allow you to remove the extra clutter from your home, without making you feel too guilty about what you've thrown away or donated.

Baby items have nostalgic appeal, true. But if you hang onto all of the items they touched growing up, they might not have room to grow up in your house.

Think about what holds special meaning (i.e. their first outfit or a blanket) and hang onto those items in a special place. But outside of a few small things, think about tossing the rest – or passing it on to a new mother who may not have the time or money to spare.

PHOTOS AND MEMORABILIA

We all look back at our past from time to time, no matter how unsentimental we claim to be. In our homes, we probably have relics of our past lives:

- Photos

- Souvenirs

- Yearbooks

- Trinkets

- Etc.

While it might be fun to amass these items over the years, if you simply put them away in a box as soon as you get them, what good are they doing you now?

One good thing to think about when you're decluttering your home is the value of your memorabilia. Right now you might be thinking about how valuable your items are, but if you're not enjoying them on a regular basis, are those items actually adding value to your life?

Instead, try to look for items in your memorabilia boxes and shelves to see if these items can be put into places where you can enjoy them – i.e. picture frames, display boxes, etc.

If you display these items, you will be able to relive the memories for longer, and the items will add decorative touches to your home – without the need for spending thousands of dollars either.

But if you're not going to display the items, and there might be other reasons for this, then think about putting them away in a box that is not going to be forgotten or ruined if it doesn't get looked at for a few years.

At the very least, try to pare down the items you own and what feels valuable to keep, even if you're not using it right at the moment.

HOUSEHOLD HAZARDOUS WASTE AND E-WASTE

In these times of innovation, it seems we have more clutter than ever before – and we're not quite sure what to do with it.

For many of us, the fact that we have no idea what to do with this clutter can cause us to just hold onto it until (someday) we figure out what we want to do with it.

Instead of avoiding dealing with household waste and electronic waste (e-waste), you need to take care of things in this manner:

- Gather the waste that you want to remove from your home.

- Talk to your local waste management company about how they want you to dispose of the items.

- Remove the rechargeable batteries – Those need to be disposed of separately in most cases.

- Take the electronic items – i.e. laptops, computers, radios, etc. – to a recycling station that accepts these items. Often, thrift stores also have the ability to recycle these items, so check to see if your local store will too.

- Place the household wastes in appropriate containers – When you talk to your local household waste management company, they will be able to tell you where to take these items and how to store them effectively.

If you have electronic waste that might not be broken or unusable, remember to take these sorts of items to the local thrift stores or charities, assuming the batteries aren't leaking or damaged.

You can't simply throw away your microwaves and other appliances either. These items can cause dangerous chemicals to be released into the ground, which can cause troubles for drinking water in the future.

One of the other common household hazardous wastes that you may be concerned about tossing in the trash is prescription medication. Though it seems as though you could just throw these items away or flush them down the toilet, this is not recommended.

Talk with your pharmacy to see if they can accept expired and unused medications. If not, then you will want to talk to the local waste management company about tossing these items properly.

In addition, if you have medications that are not accepted by any waste management companies, you might be able to secure the medications in the original container and then place that container in a bag of cat litter to help prevent the medication from leaking into the water supply.

Overall, it's best to take medications before they expire, as directed, and then you can make sure that you don't have waste to get rid of.

HOLD A YARD SALE

For many that notice they have a lot of items that are going to be tossed or removed from their home, a yard sale might seem like a good idea. This will help you to make money from the items you've already spent money on, while also making others haul off the things that you don't want to own anymore.

Know that a yard sale can be quite a commitment, but when it's done right, you can make money from the things you already want to remove from your life.

- Gather the goods – First of all, you need to gather the items that you want to sell when you're at your yard sale. These items should be in good repair and they should be able to work, as the customer expects.

- Price reasonably – Though you might want to price everything as though they were buying it new, this is not going to help you sell down your clutter. Instead, try to set prices of no more than $10, unless the item is very expensive or large.

- Be ready to haggle – Most people who come to yard sales will expect to haggle a bit with you, so you need to be ready to haggle back with them. You need to be ready to come down slightly on price or combine products in order to get a person to buy more than they might have.

- Have more than one family's things – Consider asking your neighbors to have yard sales as well. Many more shoppers will come to multi-house yard sales than might come to just one house with stuff to sell.

- Sort by category – To make sure that shoppers can easily find what they're looking for, try to organize your sale by categories like furniture, clothing, baby clothes, etc. This will help everyone go to where they want to be, and that will also help the shoppers spread out when they're shopping.

- Have testers available – Make sure that your shoppers will be able to test items that might plug in to make sure they work. After they take them home, the customer will be in charge of whether or not they continue to work.

- Advertise locally – The more that you market and advertise your yard sale, the more people will come. Try to spread the word far earlier in the week to make sure as many people show up as possible.

- Have longer hours – While most yard sales might be from 10 to 4, you might want to have extended hours on your sale, or keep your sale open until most things are sold.

A yard sale can be spread out over the course of two weekend days, or you might want to have a yard sale once a month in the summer as you will then get regular shoppers to your home.

No matter what you choose, when you can set up an effective yard sale, you can increase the possibility of removing clutter from your home – and get paid.

And some people who have problems with clutter find that yard sales make it easier for them to get rid of things.

DO YOU NEED A DUMPSTER?

If you're looking around your space and you realize you have more things to throw away than you have to save or to sell, you might start to wonder if you need a dumpster. Here are some easy questions to ask yourself before you sign up for this helpful piece of decluttering equipment:

- Do I need to throw a lot of things away?

- Do I have access to charities and other places where donations are accepted?

- Do I want to spread out my decluttering efforts?

- Do I have space in my yard/driveway for a dumpster?

- Do I have access to local dumpster services?

- Can I pay for dumpster use?

For most people, a dumpster isn't necessary as their regular trash services can accommodate the decluttering efforts, but if this isn't you, then it can help to look into these services.

Those with bigger homes, and bigger decluttering needs, will be able to throw away their clutter en masse, allowing you to have one cathartic haul away of your extra possessions.

But as these items are going to get carted off to the local landfill, it might help to try to sell or to donate as many items as possible. After all, they might be of use to others, even if they're cluttering up your space right now.

SUPPLIES YOU WILL NEED TO DECLUTTER

When you're serious about decluttering your home, you need to have some equipment around to help you with the process. Though you might have to adjust this list, depending on how much work you need to do, these are some of the essentials for making this process as simple as possible:

- Trash bags

- Sorting containers

- Tarps

- Plastic gloves

- Donation boxes

- Dumpster

The trash bags can be used to help you bag up donations and trash, but they can also help you move items from one room of your home to another, if you need to relocate items.

Sorting containers will help you to keep things separate for donation, trash, and recycling, as well as for keep piles. These are also helpful when you have the entire family pitching in on the efforts. Instead of having to show everyone where to put things, you can clearly label these containers.

Tarps can help when you want to declutter your home from top to bottom, and it's nice enough outside to put items you are sorting. You can have one tarp for each of the categories you need to sort, and then you can easily move these items back into your home or straight to the donation center or dumpster.

Plastic gloves can come in handy when you're sorting through old or potentially dangerous items. If you want to keep your hands clean, and you want to keep the items clean, these are essential.

Donation boxes can help make it easier for you to move items to the local charity, or you might need to use specific boxes if the center requires them, as some places do not accept trash bags.

In the last section, you learned about whether you might need a dumpster, and for years of clutter, this might be the tool that allows you to get rid of massive amounts of items at once.

GETTING RID OF CLUTTER ROOM BY ROOM

The clutter in your home did not magically appear (hopefully), so it will take some time to be removed from your home. By working on your home from one room to the next, you can more easily complete the task ahead of you, without feeling overwhelmed by the process.

You might want to choose one room to tackle each free day you have, helping you carefully sort through the items you have, ensuring that you make the best possible decisions.

And if you're worried about getting rid of items, the more slowly you go, the less painful it can be.

MASTER BEDROOM

Your master bedroom should be a space where you feel comfortable and relaxed. To ensure that you are getting rid of all of the items that constitute clutter, make sure you follow this plan:

- Start with the closet – This is the place where many pieces of clutter end up first, and then they're hidden until you're bursting at the seams. Take all of the clothing and other items out of this space and put them on the bed.

- Sort the clothing and closet items – Start with these items so you can put whatever you're not tossing or donating back into the closet. Plus, you'll accomplish the task, helping you to create momentum for the rest.

- Get things from under the bed – If you have a space under your bed, chances are good some things ended up there. Move those items to the top of your bed.

- Sort the under bed items – Just like your closet, start sorting the under the bed items and anything that needs to stay in your master bedroom should stay on the bed. Everything else should be put into donation boxes or tossed.

- Move to the dressers – This is another area where items are generally stored when you don't want to look at them.

- Sort through each drawer and each shelf – As you move along, you will see that you are making room for items to be organized, but this is not the point of this job just yet.

- Declutter any other spaces – Depending on what other items and storage spaces you have in your room, remove the items you don't need or want anymore, leaving only what you want to keep.

The goal for your master bedroom should be to remove anything that isn't working, isn't helping you, and that is getting in the way. You should be able to move easily in this room and everything will soon have a place where it will reside – keeping you clutter free.

KID'S BEDROOMS

Your children's bedrooms might be places where you dare not venture, as they are often messier than any other room in the house. But with the help of your kids, you can easily clean things up and begin to create organized spaces.

- Get rid of what's old – Look around to see if there are items that aren't age-appropriate anymore. Those items should go to another child or they can be donated to a charity.

- Remove small or destroyed pieces of clothing – Since your child grows quickly and they can also ruin their clothes fairly quickly, you need to remove these items from the closets and drawers as well.

- Get rid of what doesn't work – If you can't fix something or you don't want to fix something, get it out of your child's room.

- Ask your child to get rid of a few things – Though your child might not understand the reasons for decluttering, when they realize that it's okay to let go of things and give them to other children who might need them, it can encourage a clutter-free lifestyle.

- Take away any dishes or items that should be in other rooms – Since many children

47

will bring items into their room from other spaces, make sure that you return these items to their homes. This often encourages the habit of putting things back where they came from.

- Look at the walls and shelves – If there are any items that do not need to be on the walls or the shelves, remove them.

- Remove old furniture – When your child is no longer a baby, you need to remove the furniture from when they were younger. This will free up a lot of space and it will ensure that your child feels like you are encouraging them to be more grown-up.

Your child's room might be a constant source of new clutter, as they may simply not want to organize the items they have. But with time and good practice, they can learn to keep their rooms clean.

FAMILY ROOM

The family room is another area where you can have a lot of clutter, especially when you spend a lot of time in this space. The battle plan of attack for this room can look like:

- Go through the entertainment – Since this is a place where you might watch movies and play video games, it's time to look through what you have and see what you don't need anymore. Some movies might not work anymore, and other video games may not be fun for the children anymore.

- Go through the books and magazines – Many families have a lot of reading material in their family rooms as well. Try to remove the books and magazines that have already been read, or that aren't necessary anymore.

- Remove any extraneous furniture or electronics – The truth is that we often keep things in rooms because we don't really think about them all that much. For example, if your VCR isn't really in the way, you might keep it in your entertainment center. Instead, try to remove items like this that you're not using regularly. Chances are good that you won't even miss them.

- Clear off all of the surfaces – Try to remove all of the items from the flat surfaces that you can. Look at each item to see if it's necessary, and if not, then donate it or toss it.

- Clear walkways – If you find it difficult to get to certain areas of the family room, try to find ways to remove the items that are acting as obstacles. You probably don't need them anyway.

A good way to complete the decluttering in this room is to simply look around and see what you don't use anymore. When you do this as a family, you can all talk about what you like and what you don't like, helping to clear out things as a team decision.

Plus, it can help to create a rule that if you bring something into the family room, it needs to be cleared back out within a day, so as to keep the clutter to a minimum.

For bonus points, you might want to remove the many storage options you have. When you have a lot of shelves and tables, you are more likely to put things on or in them, helping to add to clutter.

This can stop now.

OFFICE

Whether you work from home or you work from a 'regular' office, you will notice that you have many opportunities for clutter. After all, when your'e working, the last thing you think about is whether your space is organized – especially when no one else but you is going to see it.

But when you have a clutter free office, you can actually be more productive. Think about what it might be like to actually be able to find the report that you need instead of spending a good hour trying to hunt for it among the piles of papers.

To work on your office, you will need to either come in early or find time where you can focus on these efforts. When this isn't possible, try to carve out small periods of time for decluttering.

- Clear off the top of the desk – The best way to begin is to look at what's on your desk right now and clear it off, separating it into toss, donate, and keep piles. Make sure that you go through every single item on this space until you only have things you NEED to keep on top of your workspace.

- Reconsider technical gear – Look at the different computer pieces and other gear you have on your desk and think about how much you use everything. If there are things that you don't use regularly, perhaps there is another space where you can store them for future use. Or perhaps there is another co-worker who might like to have the item for their job's responsibilities.

- Clear out drawers – Often, it's easy to dump things into drawers where they're out of sight and out of mind. Take out all of the items in your drawers, throwing away anything you don't need or can't identify first. Then start looking at what you need and what you can donate to the office or to a charity.

- Clear out shelves – Go to the shelves and start the same sorting process, looking carefully at handbooks and books to see if you still need these items in your office. Often, you might have things that are out of date, so those can either be recycled or they can put into another area of the office.

- Put away things that you don't need – Over the course of the year, you will use certain things often and other things not as much. Try to put away the things you don't need where you can still access them, but where they will not cause more clutter.

- Rethink your knick-knacks – Many people want to make their office space as homey as possible, but this can also look cluttered. Think about hanging a few pictures on your walls, having a few items on your desk for comfort, but limit these as much as possible. If you don't want to limit the items you have, then rotate them regularly to make it feel as though you have more on your desk than you actually do.

Your office may always be prone to having more items and clutter than it needs to, but once you've conquered your organizational patterns, you will find that it's easier to keep things under control.

And no, you don't need to have a messy desk in order to look like you're keeping yourself out of trouble.

KITCHEN

One area of the home where clutter is often accepted is the kitchen, but why is this? When you have a cluttered kitchen, you might:

- Create sanitation problems

- Buy foods you already have/waste the foods you've already bought

- Forget where certain cooking items are

- End up going out to eat because you don't want to cook in your kitchen

And these are just a few of the problems that clutter can cause in your kitchen. To make sure that you're creating a place where cooking can actually occur:

- Clear the counters – Start by clearing off the counters as this is where the clutter accumulates first. Remove dishes that need to be washed, items that need to be put away, etc.

- Get rid of expired/suspicious foods – Many of us don't have the time or the inspiration to look at the foods we have, so we end up with foods that are not usable after a while. Try to remove these from your home quickly, tossing what is suspicious as it is better to get rid of something than to 'enjoy' food poisoning.

- Donate unused appliances – If you haven't used an appliance in six months, chances are good that you probably won't use it. Get rid of it or give it to a friend so you know you can borrow it if you do end up wanting to use it.

- Keep only 8 to 12 table settings – Many people have far more dishes and cups than they will ever need to use at a party. While this might be helpful for the environment, it can also cause you to have more clutter in your kitchen. Instead, remove any extra place settings you have.

- Get rid of mismatching dishes – Though you might have some cups and plates that you hang onto for sentimental reasons, try to remove any other dishes that do not 'go' with the rest of your set.

- Get rid of kids dishes – If your kids have been out of the house for a while, it's safe to get rid of their dishes and their bottles. You can always donate them to families who might be struggling to buy these items on their own.

- Get rid of larger pots and pans – Unless you're cooking a lot of big meals, you probably don't need to have larger pots and pans in your home. They are only taking up space, which can be used to take care of clutter.

Getting rid of clutter in the kitchen begins with assessing what you have and what you actually need and use.

Though you might not be able to guess what your entertaining needs for the next year might be, the more that you can look at your kitchen items, the more you can weed out the things you don't really need.

And if you need to purchase something in the future, then you can always go back and do so. But in most cases, you probably won't miss the items you tossed or donated.

DINING ROOM

If you look around your dining room right now, you'll notice that this room is very cluttered or not cluttered at all – depending on how often you use it. In either case, this can become a place where you store things if you don't have anywhere else to put them.

And if you don't use the room that often, this room can become filled with items that seem to pile up to the ceiling after a while.

To declutter your dining room, you need to:

- Remove extra dishes – Most people will have table settings for more than one occasion and for as many people as they might think will come over for special occasions.

- Remove extra dishes – If you have a gravy boat that you rarely use or a tureen (and other such pieces of dining ware), you should put these into a box and into storage. These dishes don't need to be sitting out.

- Consider what you use – The best way to declutter your dining room is to think about the things you actually use when you have people over and what you might be able to donate to others. If you haven't used certain dishes in a while, it's time to pass them on to someone else or give them away to a charity.

The dining room can be a sparse room if you don't regularly eat in it. And if you find that clutter still makes its way onto the table, you need to remove it as soon as it is found.

Right now, if there is clutter on the table:

- Sort it into piles – Keep, donate, toss/recycle

- Put the appropriate items back into their appropriate rooms

This simple process allows you the opportunity to have only the items you may need in the room.

BATHROOMS

You might not realize this, but the bathroom is one of the rooms in your home right now where you will spend most of your life. As a result, you might be storing a lot of additional items in this room without even realizing it.

A good way to approach decluttering in this room is to:

- Pull everything out of the drawers and cupboards

- Sort items by keep, toss, donate/recycle

- Look at the bottles of beauty care products – If a bottle has an expiration date, toss the item, or rinse out the bottle and recycle the bottle.

- Look for items you don't use – Remove any items that you don't use anymore, and get rid of them. If they're unopened, you might be able to return them to a store or give them to others.

- Remove anything that isn't used in the bathroom – If you don't use an item in the bathroom, it should not be stored there.

Try to make your bathroom space into an area where you only have the items you need to clean yourself or to make yourself healthy. Anything else can be discarded or moved to a new location.

In addition, it can help to remove any extra stockpiles of toilet paper and other related items. While having some extras is a good idea, most of the backup products can be put into a storage closet and brought into the bathroom when you're actually out of the item.

SPARE ROOMS

Many people will have additional rooms in their home, i.e. dens, that will also accumulate clutter because they're not used as often as other rooms. Just as with any other space in your home, you can begin by sorting into the three or four piles.

The next way to attempt to declutter the spare rooms is to make sure that you're removing items that should be in other rooms. Just take these items, put them into a pile, and when you're done decluttering the room, then move these items to the appropriate location.

It can help as you are decluttering your extra rooms to think about what the purpose of the room might be. This pre-thinking will help you when you begin to organize, as you will know what items need to stay in the rooms, and which items should be removed entirely.

Other tips include:

- Remove extra furniture – If you have furniture in your spare rooms that has been covered in clutter, chances are good that you don't need those pieces of furniture anymore. Perhaps it's time to toss it or to donate it?

- Consider extra unused items – Since spare rooms can be places where you store additional items that don't fit anywhere else, or that aren't useful anymore, make sure to move these items out.

Spare rooms can become extra storage areas, but when they begin to only fulfil that purpose in your life, that's when clutter can start to seep out into other areas of your home too.

CLOSETS

Many of us will use our closets as places where we can hide the clutter we want to hide. Though this is certainly helpful when company comes over, it's not very helpful for our bigger organizational goals.

Instead, you will want to start removing items from your closet in order to make space for a system. The organization system will help you actually find what you're looking for.

- Start the piles – keep, donate, toss, and recycle.

- Get rid of anything that doesn't fit – If you're holding onto clothing that you used to fit into or that you want to fit into, this isn't a bad thing, but it can cause clutter. It's a better idea to only store clothing items that fit in your closet.

- Get rid of anything that's out of style, ripped, or stained – To make things easier on you, try to remove any pieces of clothing that you don't wear. These items will be easy to find, as they're generally far in the back, and you may have completely forgotten about them.

- Remove non-clothing items – When you're decluttering a clothing closet, make sure to remove anything that's not associated with the outfits you wear.

- Linen closets – When you store blankets, sheets, and towels in a closet, you need to make sure that you're keeping this closet free from clutter. This might mean you need to remove anything that isn't a linen, in your opinion. In addition, remove anything that's stained, ripped, or old.

- Coat closets – Just as in your clothing closet, when you get to your coat closet, make sure to remove anything that might be out of date or anything that doesn't fit you well. Try things on to see if you still like the style of your coats, and donate what doesn't work anymore. You may also want to think about how often you wear the coats in your closet, and try to keep only one for each season in which you might need something slightly warmer.

- Craft closets – In some houses, you might have a craft closet where you store things for art projects with the kids, or you might store things for decorating or gift wrapping. In these closets, make sure that you remove anything that you don't use or that is ripped or soiled. It can also help to remove anything that doesn't work for your needs anymore (i.e. glue guns, Velcro, etc.).

- Kids closets – A child's closet can become overrun with items that are old and unneeded anymore. Start by looking at all of the sizes in the closet and removing anything that doesn't fit your child anymore. Then look at what remains to see what is too stained or too soiled to be worn. You will also want to look at the shoes that are in the closet to see if they can be donated or thrown away.

No matter what kinds of closets you have, make sure that you are trying to remove all of the items that don't serve your purposes anymore. In doing so, you will free up the space, and the next step of organizing will be much easier.

LAUNDRY ROOM

Often, when you use your laundry room or area, you might not even think about the clutter you are creating. Since this area is often closed away from the rest of the house, it's easy to forget what's hiding in there.

To declutter this space:

- Remove extra socks – One of the most common sources of clutter are extra socks that seem to have lost their partners in the wash. Remove all of these extra socks from the area and use them as rags, or donate them to someone else who might not care about having a matching pair.

- Keep only laundry items in the space – No matter what you have in your laundry room, it's a good idea to remove anything that might not be associated with washing and drying clothing. Anything else needs to go back to the room where it belongs.

- Remove clean clothing – If you have piles of clean clothing in your laundry area, you will want to remove those piles and put the clothing in the closet or drawer from which it came.

- Clear away old laundry products – It's easy to have too many laundry products in a laundry room, so remove anything that you don't use or don't need anymore.

Your laundry room should be a space in which it is simple to get your laundry done, and keep it clean. Most of the battle in this room is because clean clothing isn't put away immediately, but once you have this space organized, this will not be a concern – and neither will clutter.

GARAGE/BASEMENT/ATTIC

While it's true that your garage, basement, and/or attic are all spaces where you can easily store more items, the likelihood of clutter is exponential.

Out of sight, out of mind, for most people.

To make sure that you're using these spaces efficiently, it's a good idea to:

- Remove anything dangerous – This task applies mainly to the garage. When you're looking around your garage, think about what you can remove that might be dangerous, i.e. old gas cans, paint cans, etc. If you have dangerous chemicals in this space, do your best to remove them and then dispose of them properly, per your waste management resources.

- Remove anything that leaks – If you lift anything in these rooms that leaks, it might be a sign that you need to remove these items from the space. Though they might not be dangerous, anything that leaks will eventually run out of its contents, and until then, this item is just taking up space.

- Consider what you use/don't use – Look around the room and think about the last time that you used the items you are

68

storing in these rooms. If you haven't used the items in over a year, it might be time to donate them to someone who will. And think about how many times you will continue to use the items you still have in these spaces. If you had a lawn, but then switched it out for decorative rocks, for example, you can get rid of your lawnmower or other associated tools.

- Remove heavier/delicate items – If you have heavy or delicate items in your home's lesser frequented spaces, chances are good they will never leave the room, creating clutter. Remove any items that might not be necessary to keep in these spaces, and consider whether you need them at all if you never look at them.

The main key to decluttering your attic, garage, and basement is to look at things that might not be useful, as these are areas where less useful things tend to hang out.

Get rid of things that aren't adding value to your life, and you will find the extra space is all the more helpful than the things you donated or got rid of.

PETS

Pets are lovely friends and companions in families, but their things can also begin to add clutter to your home. Instead of hanging onto everything they might need, it's time to reassess the pet clutter.

- Think about safety – Because you want your pet to be safe and healthy, it can help to think about how their safety is being impacted by the things you own. Things that your pet shouldn't be using because of their size or health limitations should be removed from your home.

- Consider expiration dates – On food and other items for your pets, you will find expiration dates. Anything that is expired should be tossed out or taken to your vet to dispose of properly.

- Look at old toys – Look over the toys that your pets have played with to see if they will still be able to have more playtime in them. When a toy is mangled or smaller pieces are starting to come off, it's time to toss the toys.

- Put all pet things in one area – Make sure that you find all of the pet items from your home and put them into one area when you declutter. You may find that you have more items than you realized, which will encourage you to get rid of more.

Your pets are beloved creatures, but this doesn't mean their items need to clutter up your home.

THE COMPUTER AND EMAIL

For many people, the clutter that's on your computer and in your email box might be a nuisance, but it seems to be a nuisance that you can't avoid. Or can you?

The idea of an inbox and a desk without any chaos cluttering it up may sound like a dream, but with a few simple fixes, you can make sure the clutter is limited.

- Empty the trash – The first thing you can do with your email or your actual computer desk is to empty your trash bins. When you do this, you will make sure that you're not holding onto anything that you already decided to throw away.

- Sort everything on your desktop – On your virtual and your literal desktops, make sure you clear everything off and sort these items into keep, delete, and store.

- Delete old files – Yes, your computer does not have unlimited space in which to keep the things you want to keep. Delete the old files that you don't need anymore.

For your email, it's a good idea to remove anything that you don't use anymore, or that you don't need to keep. You will also want to delete any emails you have sitting around that you haven't answered in more than a month.

Chances are good that the other person will email you again if they really want to hear from you.

In addition, it can help to unsubscribe yourself from any mailing lists you might be on, as well as any cancel any subscriptions you might have. This will dramatically cut down on the clutter you receive, and it will free up your time.

HOW TO ORGANIZE ROOM BY ROOM

Once you've gotten your clutter under control, you need to start organizing what remains. Though you can take the clutter away, if you don't find some sort of system that works for you, you may end up with a cluttered space once more.

The key to organization is to make sure that everything has its own place to reside. So, when you use something, you can immediately put it back in its place when you're done – keeping things clean.

As with any advice, there are many ways in which you can approach the organization in your home. In this section, you will learn more about the organizational tips that work best for most families, and you can figure out what works best for you as you continue to live your clutter-free life.

MASTER BEDROOM

In the master bedroom, you will want to think of the space as having zones:

- Clothing

- Entertainment

- Sleep

These three zones are simple enough to manage, and it allows you to sort the items you own into these areas. Clothing will go into the closet and into the drawers, while entertainment might be on the shelves or in a nightstand.

Sleeping items should be on the bed.

If you stick to this sort of system, you will be able to arrange all of your items into places where you can not only use the items you need when you need them, but you will be able to put them back quickly.

You can also:

- Invest in a closet organizer – If you find that your closet is hard to control or that you don't have enough space for hanging, the clutter can come back more easily. Instead, look into an organizer that gives you shelves for shoes, more bars for hanging items, etc. This will help you manage the items you have as well, since you will only have so many areas to use for the remaining items you own.

- Look into drawer organizers – When you have smaller items that need to be put into your bedroom drawers, it can help to get drawer dividers. For example, you can use these dividers to hold jewelry, socks, and underwear so that you can easily find what you need, and you can keep everything in its place.

- Use an underbed organizer – If you have items that you need ot have in your bedroom, but you don't need to use everyday, you can invest in an underbed box or organizer. This box will hold any extra blankets, for example, or it can help you with your summer and winter clothing exchange.

Speaking of clothing, if you do have a lot of summer and winter clothing, it might be a good idea to store the clothing you're not using during specific months. This will keep your closet organized, and it will help you find weather-appropriate outfits for any time of year.

You're not necessarily getting rid of any clothing in this way. However, you may find that when the seasons change, you're less likely to wear certain items that you might have worn the year before – merely because you forgot about them.

KID'S BEDROOMS

While you might be tempted to say that your child's room can remain disorganized until they move out, this is not going to teach them how to be neat and organized.

Instead, you can turn keeping their room into a game that allows them to build better habits as they grow up and own more things.

- Toy box – When children are younger, it can help to have a large toy box into which everything needs to go at the end of the day. If the toys are too numerous to put in the box, then it's a sign that your child needs to get rid of a few items.

- Everything has a hanger – To encourage children to keep their clothing in the closet, make sure that every piece of clothing they own has a hanger. Tell your child that this is a game to make sure that the hangers end up in the closet so they can sleep at the end of the day.

- Label the drawers – When children are able to read, you can label the drawers of their dressers to show them where certain items go when they are clean or not being used.

- Pictures on the containers – And when your children are younger, you can include pictures of what should go into different containers in their room.

- Organize before bed – Though it might seem easier to just have everything declutter and organize on the weekends, you want to save that time for other family events. Instead, spend ten minutes each night before bed putting things away to keep the rooms clean.

Even if your children have had troubles managing their clutter in the past, this is a good time to turn over a new leaf and show them that organization is possible.

Ask your children for suggestions about how they would organize their things too, so everyone can get involved in the process.

FAMILY ROOM

In the family room, there are several ways in which to organize in order to minimize clutter and to keep the area inviting to use when company comes over.

- Use DVD and CD folders – Instead of having boxes of DVDs and CDs around, try using folders into which the discs can be placed. These take up less room and they're easier to manage.

- Have a box of games and other entertainment pieces – If your family is interested in games, have a box into which all of these items go, and then push that box out of sight when it's not in use.

- Create shelves for different members of the family – This will help everyone be responsible for a part of the room, without having to organize everything.

- Have one piece of entertainment furniture – The more spaces you have to place things, the more likely it is that you will put clutter on these open areas. Instead, try to have just one piece of entertainment related furniture – i.e. an entertainment center. If you limit what you can use for movies and games, you will not have as many in the room.

- Have a clear off policy – Whoever is in the room last will need to make sure they adhere to the clean off policy. This means that they need to remove everything that's been left on the surfaces of the family room. Or you can have the entire family commit to taking away anything they brought in with them when they entered the family room.

The family room is simple enough to keep clean when you come up with a few rules and organization systems.

If your family room is larger and holds more items, then you might need to have more than one piece of furniture to hold books, for example. This is fine, but make sure that the books can always fit comfortably in the space allotted to them.

OFFICE

The office area of a home can be challenging to organize, especially when the person working in there is constantly busy. But there are many good ways in which you can organize this space, allowing the person using it to be more productive.

In the office, it's a good idea to create zones.

- Active work

- Passive work

- Reference

The active work area is generally the computer area. This is the space in which the person does most of their work activities during the day, and they will spend most of their time there.

This space should include office supplies that are in easy reach, using cups and boxes to contain these items. If there are drawers on the desk, the top drawer should contain all of the items the person in the office might need to use most days.

A filing cabinet or second drawer can serve as the filing drawer, if needed. In this area, you will keep papers that you need to access regularly.

On the desk itself, you should only have the items that you use often – the computer and keyboard, perhaps a backup hard drive. Other items like a printer and phone should go in a separate area, as this will allow for more desk space.

A separate filing cabinet can be helpful for office papers, though it might not be necessary to have it out all the time. Instead, you might want to have this piece of equipment in the closet where it can be utilized, but not until the papers are needed.

Another great place to keep calendars and other items you might need to reference during the day is the sliding keyboard shelf that comes with some desks. If you're not using this space for a keyboard (and many don't), use it to keep things you need to review regularly.

The passive part of the office is the place where you might keep books you need to reference or other items you use some of the time – i.e. a scanner, fax, etc.

In this area, it's a good idea to have supportive supplies for those pieces of machinery, as well as a notepad to keep track of what you are doing with the supplies you have out. If you're not using these items, and you don't plan to use them for a while, it might be better to put them into a closet.

To keep track of things you need to do:

- Wipe off boards

- Cork boards

These can be hung on the wall or attached magnetically to a filing cabinet. And they can store notes you need to have, as well as business cards and other pieces of paper that you might lose in piles on your desk.

The main key to organization your office is to have a system that will reduce the possibility of clutter. To do this, all you need to do is:

- Make decisions quickly – Whenever you get something in your office, decide immediately how you will use it. Whether it's going on the active or passive part of your office, make sure you decide as soon as you have the item in your hand.

- Clean your desk at night – At the end of each office shift, make sure that you clean off the surface of your desk to make sure you're keeping things neat and that you're not losing anything in the shuffle of the work you do.

- Do a thorough clean once a month – It can help every month when you organize your financial statements to organize your office too. Get rid of anything that you don't need, file anything you need to file, etc.

The office is a space that simply needs to have a clear process of what goes where and how to handle new items when they come in.

KITCHEN

To organize your kitchen, it's a good idea to look into the idea of zones again.

- Preparation

- Cooking

- Serving

- Cleaning

While you might have more space and more opportunities for zones, these three will get you started.

In the preparation area, you will have all the mixing bowls and other items you might need to prepare the foods and meals you make. This should be close to the waste basket and the sink. You can also have the spices here and any other items that you might need for food prep, including appliances.

In the cooking area, you will have the stove and oven area, but this should be close to the preparation area since you might need to add more spices when you're heating foods up.

The serving area is where you have your dishes and other items onto and into which you place finished foods. You can also have silverware here so that guests can serve themselves.

In the cleaning area, this would be where you can clean things up – the sink, the dishwasher, etc.

So, to organize your kitchen, you will want to move all of the items that you've already pared down into their target zones. All of the things you use frequently should be within reach, while things you don't use often can be put into higher cupboards or down low to keep them out of the way, but still in the kitchen.

Other organizational ideas include:

- Pot racks – If you don't have a lot of room for the pots you will use when you're cooking, then you might want to use pot racks that hang above your stove or on a wall. From there, you can hang the pots and have them in easy reach.

- Knife blocks – Having all of your 'good' knives in a block on the counter is much neater and it also keeps the knives safely within reach.

- Drawer dividers – Although you probably already have these in place, it can help to have dividers in your drawers to allow for the different kinds of silverware to be easy to find.

- Different drawers for different items – Try to have a drawer for your regular silverware, as well as one for the things you need for cooking. This will allow you to keep things neat, and it will allow you to have space to move around to get the things you need when someone else needs to be in another drawer at the same time.

- Designated shelves – It can help to label certain shelves in your kitchen cupboards to ensure that things that get organized on the shelves will return to where they came from. You can label the insides of the cupboards so no one else but you can see it.

- Lazy Susans – If you have a lot of spices and deeper cupboards, you might want to invest in lazy Susans, which allow you to put spices and other bottles on these platforms, which can then be spun around until you find what you need.

- Vertical storage – Some find that they can utilize their larger cupboards more effectively by adding shelves or platforms that allow you to have different levels of storage instead of stacking everything on top of each other.

You can find a number of different methods of organization tools at your local supply stores, but these ideas can get your organizational system started, and from there, you can add more tools as you find you're getting used to the clutter-free life.

DINING ROOM

Organizing a dining room is simple when you have the table as the central focus. Once you have that table in place, here are some simple ways to store the rest of your belongings:

- Use a small china cabinet – It can help to invest in a small china cabinet as this can help you store the special dishes you might want to use on holidays and other occasions. Just be certain to only have the smallest amount possible as you want to make sure that you're keeping things as clutter-free as possible. Or you can choose to store your special dishes elsewhere, freeing you from having to have this special piece of furniture.

- Keep only the bare essentials – It's true. The best way to have a clutter-free house is to make sure that you only have what you absolutely need to function in a room. If you don't use your dining room that often, then this makes things easier. But if you eat in your dining room each night, you might need a few more items to have what you need, when you need it.

- Set the table – One way to have the items you need in place is to set the table ahead of time, and have this prepared for each time you sit down to the table. It sounds strange, but having placemats and glasses out on the table will seem like clutter, but when you have these out, you also don't have space for other items that aren't food-related. And you will be able to have a decorative space too.

The dining room doesn't have to have anything more on the table but a vase of flowers or some other decorative centerpiece, so why not keep things simple by storing nothing in this room?

BATHROOMS

In order to organize the bathroom, you will want to think about the different items you need to keep in this space:

- Cleaning supplies – You will want to clean the bathroom regularly, so you will want to have these supplies in the space to make this as easy as possible. Have these supplies in a bucket so you can have everything in one place where you can easily grab it and use it.

- Hair care – For those who are interested in styling their hair, it can help to have one drawer dedicated to these products, or another bucket under the sink. This will keep all of the products in the same place. Hair styling tools like dryers and curling irons can also go into these places when they're cooled off, instead of sitting on the counter.

- Face care – Face care products should have their own section too, helping to keep these in reach for the morning and evening, while also helping to keep track of what you have and what you might need to buy the next time you're at a store.

- Tooth care – Toothbrushes, toothpaste, and floss, should be put into an area that is beside the sink. Some prefer to put these items in a drawer, out of sight, so that's an option. To keep them from cluttering up the counter, just make sure that everyone has a place for their toothbrush to reside, and then put away the toothpaste and floss when finished.

- Body care – Soap and other body care products that are used in the bathtub should be placed on a shelf in the tub or in a hanging shower rack. If these items don't need to be used every time you're in the shower, then they should be put under the sink.

- Towels – Towels should hang from hooks on the back of the bathroom door or you can install additional towel rack bars to make sure everyone gets one, or everyone gets to share one if you're short on space.

- Toilet paper – A good way to add space for toilet paper is to use a roll holder beside the toilet. This is a bar that simply corrals your TP until you need to replace the roll, and it helps you keep track of when you need to bring in more supplies.

When your bathroom is very small, it can help to invest in a storage piece that can sit behind and over your toilet. This can add some storage space for towels, as well as for toilet paper and other items you need to have stocked, but that you don't need all the time.

If you have many people in your family, it can also be a good idea for each person to have their own shower caddy or bucket that's filled with their items. This way, they can bring this bucket into the bathroom when they need to use it, but then they can take it out to keep the area clutter-free.

SPARE ROOMS

The main reason why spare rooms tend to get cluttered quickly is that they don't always have a main purpose to them. Instead of just having spare rooms around, give them a new life by giving them a direction to their use.

For example, you can turn one into the library, where you store your books and other learning tools. Or you can turn a room into an exercise room, so all of the exercise equipment is there.

Try to find a way to categorize the rooms that you have in addition to your bedrooms. When you do this, you will be able to organize more effectively.

- Create zones of use – As in any room, start to picture how you will use the room and lay out the items you have accordingly. This will help you understand what needs to go where. From there, you can add dressers, shelves, and other organizational tools that will corral the items needed for those tasks.

- Consider storage second – If you don't have a clear direction for the room that you are trying to organize, make sure that you use it for storage second. What this means is that you don't want to just turn it into a storage area because you can't think of anything else. Use the closets as storage for now, but make it a goal to have a greater purpose for the room.

Spare rooms can be tricky, especially when you don't have a reason for them. Instead of looking at this as a clutter 'gray area,' think about all of the ways that you can use these extra rooms to enhance your life, and not just collect your extra stuff.

LAUNDRY ROOM

When you need to organize your laundry room, you need to go back to the zone idea once more.

- Clean

- Dry

- Iron/Other tasks

The first part of your laundry room should be focused on cleaning supplies, like detergent, as well as stain removers. Think of this as the first step that your clothes will have to take when they enter the room. The clothes should also be separated here with a series of different baskets (light, dark, mixed, special loads) or a laundry sorter.

The next area should have dryer sheets and softener, as needed. This will be the place where you transfer the laundry from the wash to the dryer, obviously.

Of course, this system can be confusing when the washer and dryer are stacked on each other, so these zones may need to be combined.

If possible, you should also have another area where you might iron and fold your clothing. You can attach an iron to a wall or to the back of a door to have this readily available, even in

96

smaller areas. And that board can double as a space to fold clothes.

When you're done with the laundry that's been cleaned and folded, it should be removed from the laundry room as quickly as possible. This will allow the room to stay neat and clean, while also making sure you don't become confused about what's clean and what's dirty still.

CLOSETS

While it might seem simple enough to just go out and buy a closet organizer system, this is not the only way to make sure that your closets stay clutter free.

- Store what you don't use – If you don't have a regular use for something in your home, then go ahead and store it in the garage or attic. This will help cut down on clutter in closets, especially clutter that doesn't help you in your everyday life.

- Use crates – To separate different types of items in your closets, it can help to use small plastic crates. You can see through them and you can pull the out when you need to access what's inside of them.

- Stackable plastic containers – Plastic containers with lids can be helpful when you have space in your closet to stack items. With these containers, you can label the contents and you can move them around as needed.

- Put what you need in reach – It's always a good rule in closets to put the items that you need in reach, while putting other items out of reach. On the very top shelves, place extra towels and sheets, while the shelves at your eye level and arm level will have the things you need.

- Hanging strategy – When your closet needs to have things hanging up, make sure to hang the things you use most in the middle, and push other items out to the far sides. This will help you be able to find what you're looking for.

When you have an organization strategy in your closets, you will be able to create more room for items you need, while also being able to access the things that you will use. And when you can more easily access what you use, there is a smaller risk of you throwing things around and creating a mess in the process.

You can just use what you need, put it back, and then move on with your day.

GARAGE/BASEMENT/ATTIC

When you're organizing the other areas of your home where you don't venture often, you need to remember that the conditions in these areas are a little different – i.e. humidity, space limitations, etc.

To make sure you're keeping these areas organized, it can help to use the same sorts of systems of labeling and container management.

- Use labeled plastic containers – You may want to invest in a series of plastic tubs that will allow you to put items into the containers safely. These containers will keep things protected and the items can then be stored for longer periods of time between uses. Using different colors for different items can also help you when you need to find something.

- Use stackable crates – In the garage especially where you might have sporting goods and other needed items, stackable crates can help you keep things in reach, but also in places where they can be easily identifed.

- Avoid cardboard boxes – While cardboard boxes can be helpful, they can also become damaged easily. Try to avoid these and replace them with plastic containers that are more sturdy.

- Consider shelving – Using shelves can also help to organize items and keep them within reach, especially in the garage. When you have tools and other pieces of equipment, you can keep like items together, allowing you to easily find what you need and see what you might need to buy in the future.

In these more hidden areas of your home, look for ways to group items by use – i.e. lawn care items, car washing items, etc. This can also help with the minimization of clutter, while also allowing you to find what you need right when you require it.

PETS

To organize pet items, it can help to have a container for each pet, if they have a lot of items that they use.

- Food – Have plastic containers into which you can place bags of food. This will help keep the food fresh, and free from critters that might be in your home (including your pets!).

- Toys – Another plastic container of toys can help you organize what pet gets what, and these containers can help when you have others take care of your pets when you are away.

- Medications – You will want to store medications like flea treatments in a separate area. This will allow you to have a space where you can see if you need to restock your items, and you can keep these items out of reach of those who should not touch the items without supervision.

- Travel items – Another plastic container can include the travel items your pets might need, allowing you to bring them with you on a vacation, or to give them to someone who is caring for your pets in your home.

Have a separate area in the garage where you keep your pet supplies, or you might want to have a larger drawer available near the area where your pets eat for easier access.

THE COMPUTER AND EMAIL

To organize your computer, it can help to take a few different approaches:

- Have three desktop folders – When you have to keep track of different documents, you might want to have three different folders on your desktop area – to do, to think about, and to file away. These folders will allow you to keep track of what needs to be done, and you can clear them out as you complete tasks.

- Sync your items offline – While you might not think of organization and backup systems as being the same, often clutter on your desk or on your computer accumulates because you are afraid you will lose something. Invest in a system that automatically backs up your virtual files and scan any paper documents you don't want to lose, saving them onto a flash drive or extra hard drive.

When you want to organize your email, it can help to have a similar system of filing:

- Have separate folders – Try to organize your emails into things that you answer, things that you need to keep, and things you need to think about. This will help you keep your emails in places where you can easily find them. It can also help to create email folders for specific tasks and projects so you can return to them often.

- Funnel email into one account – If you've gotten disorganized because you have multiple email accounts, it can help to have the email funnel into just one account. This will allow you to see everything at once, dealing with it as it arrives instead of in smaller batches where things can get lost.

- Use a large email account – It can also help to have an email provider that is able to handle large volumes of emails, like Gmail. This way, you can save as much as you like, and you can return to it via the search option instead of trying to organizing into folders all at once.

Your computer and email areas might be a bit overwhelming at first, especially if you do your personal and professional communication in this way, but over time, you will find a system that works for you.

DOWNSIZING

One of the best ways to keep your life clutter free and organized is to downsize your space. When you have less space in which to keep things, it tends to keep you more honest about what you should own and what you might want to throw away.

There are two main situations in which downsizing can be indicated, and you can take these two situations as opportunities to be more effective with your decluttering.

KIDS HAVE MOVED OUT

When the kids have moved out, you might find that you have rooms where you don't need to have certain items anymore. While your children may have brought many of their possessions with them to school or to a new apartment, you need to still handle the decluttering and organization of these rooms so they don't become storage areas.

- Give away what isn't needed – If your children don't want the things that remain in their old rooms, focus on giving these items away to those who might need them.

- Put possible needed items into storage – When your kids have left items that they can't move at the present time, it can help to put these items into a separate storage facility where they can be accessed later. Have a time limit in which you will store these items so your children know when they need to make a final decision on what to do with these items (or else they need to start paying for the storage costs).

- Keep sentimental items... and give them as gifts – At first, you might tempted to keep everything as is, since your child might come back for a visit. But in time, you will want to box up the more sentimental items and try to use them in your decorations in the home. Or you might want to start giving away these items at the holidays to your children, and then they can decide whether they want to keep them or give them away.

Once your children have moved out, try to create new spaces from their bedrooms. You might still want to use these rooms as guest rooms, but keep things as minimal as possible.

MOVING TO A SMALLER HOME

In other situations, you might decide to move to a smaller home out of desire or out of financial necessity. To make sure that you're keeping things clutter free and organized, here are some tips you can use:

- Get rid of what won't fit – Before you move, take measurements of your new home to find out what pieces of furniture will fit and which will not. You will find that you can't keep everything, and when you realize you also don't have the space for it, it can make it easier to donate items or to give them away to others.

- Decide on usefulness – Think about each item that you want to bring with you and consider its usefulness. You might be moving to an area where certain things aren't needed anymore, which can help you to limit what you want to pack.

- Create a set number of moving boxes – Instead of moving everything that you own and deciding when you get to the new place, set a limit of boxes that you will bring with you. Or you can decide on a certain size of moving vehicle. If things don't fit in these areas, then you need to get rid of them.

- Consider storage for larger items – When you have some items you don't want to get rid of, consider storage for a certain period of time. At the end of this time frame, then you will get rid of the items that are no longer used.

- Get rid of what you can find elsewhere – If you have a lot of books, for example, make sure to get rid of those books you can find at a library or online. This will help you to downsize, without actually having to give up the things you love. Most books can be found at local libraries and if you need to read them again, you can just borrow them instead of moving them from home to home.

Downsizing can be a great opportunity for you to also look at the items in your home that never left their original moving boxes. If things are still in those sorts of boxes, then it might be time to let them go.

Finally, when you're downsizing, remember what's more important to you, space or having everything that you one owned follow you to your new location.

HOW TO MAINTAIN A CLUTTER FREE HOUSE

Even though you might be highly motivated to clean up your home and to organize everything, you might begin to lose this motivation after a while – especially when clutter has become a habit.

Just like any habit you have, it will take time to break this cycle and it might take time for you to become a more organized person. But you can maintain your new clean home, with a little effort.

KEEPING THE KID'S TOYS ORGANIZED

A common concern when it comes to maintaining order in a home is toys. Children aren't necessarily interested in cleaning up after themselves, so it needs to become a habit, or just something they now do as a part of their days.

- Have clean up times – Every day, it will be good for the children to put away the toys they have used. If this is built into the end of the day, it will become as natural as brushing their teeth, especially when the entire family is doing the same thing.

- Have places for things to be put – Always have places where the toys need to be put at the end of the day. This will make things easier and as the children grow older, they will need less supervision during this chore.

- Do a once-a-month clean out – Every month, make sure that you have a time to clean out the items and reassess the clutter you have. If a child, for example, has received a toy, then they should learn to get rid of one or two old toys to make sure that things aren't getting out of control again.

- Reward organization – When a child is able to keep their space organized, they

111

should be rewarded with some sort of privilege or an allowance. While in time you may want your children to simply clean up because they want to, it can help to create a reward system until the habit is formed.

Children may not seem to want to be organized, but when it's framed as helping their parents, they are more likely to try.

Of course, you need to set the example for them. Clean up after yourself each night, and they will follow suit.

MAINTAINING ORGANIZATION

To ensure that all of your hard work and decluttering efforts last long-term, you need to follow a few simple rules.

- Evaluate each purchase – Each time you buy something, think about how you will use it and what it will mean to have it in your home. This will allow you the chance to make sure that you're only amassing things you actually will use or have a clear intention for using, instead of buying things that will just end up in a pile.

- Don't hang anything over anything else – While it can be tempting to throw coats and other items over couches and exercise equipment, instead make sure that you put items where they belong, unless you're going to move the item quickly.

- Have a clear counter rule – Every day, you should look at the surfaces in your home and remove anything that might be sitting in these areas. This will help you begin to realize that you should put items away once they come into your house, instead of having to spend time cleaning up when you want to be doing other things.

- Remove items when new items come in – Just like in your kid's room, make sure that each time you get something you're also getting rid of something else. This will help to reduce the overall potential for new clutter and chaos.

- Spend time each day on decluttering – Every day, you should spend about fifteen minutes decluttering your home. This doesn't mean you need to get out the piles system, but you do want to make sure you're attacking clutter before it takes over your life. Spend a little time in the morning and night, and you will find it's easier to keep a handle on the possessions you have.

- Put items back where you found them – After you are done using something, make sure to put it back where you found it. If you don't know where something goes, make sure to ask where someone else put it so that there's a clear system of organization.

- Return items to their specific rooms – If you don't know and you can't find out where something belongs, it's a good idea to return items at least to their specific rooms of use. This will help ensure the item can be easily found again.

- Re-evaulate your organization system once a year – Every year, think about how you have organized your home, and whether these systems have worked. If not, then find new ways to organize your items, or stick with the system you have in place.

Maintaining order becomes second nature when you realize just how helpful being clutter-free and organized is. The more that you begin to focus on minimizing clutter, the less of a problem it will be.

CONCLUSION

No matter how messy you think your life is right now, you can remove the clutter. All you have to do is to look at the reasons why you might be holding onto clutter:

- Worry about not having enough

- Sentimental attachment

- Worry about wasting money

- Wanting to have lots of the best things

- Depression

- Denial

- Grief

- Being raised by people with clutter

Use a simple system for determining what should stay and what should go:

- Sort into piles

- Decide on the value of an item

- Decide where it goes

And then organize for each room of your house.

- Consider where you will use the item

- Think about what you need to use regularly

- Use storage containers to create spaces for each item

Finally, you need to maintain the order in your home:

- Put things back after you use them

- Create times each day for decluttering and re-organization

- Make organization a habit for the entire family

When you begin to see the results of your organization efforts, and you realize how much time, money, and stress you're saving, you'll see that a clutter free life is the best way to life.

After all, you don't want clutter controlling your life anymore, do you?

And the good news is – it doesn't have to.

Did you find this book helpful? If so, please tell us what you thought at:

http://www.booksurl.com/declutterbook

DISCLOSURES AND DISCLAIMERS

All trademarks and service marks are the properties of their respective owners. All references to these properties are made solely for editorial purposes. Except for marks actually owned by the Author or the Publisher, no commercial claims are made to their use, and neither the Author nor the Publisher is affiliated with such marks in any way.

Unless otherwise expressly noted, none of the individuals or business entities mentioned herein has endorsed the contents of this book.

Limits of Liability & Disclaimers of Warranties

Because this book is a general educational information product, it is not a substitute for professional advice on the topics discussed in it.

The materials in this book are provided "as is" and without warranties of any kind either express or implied. The Author and the Publisher disclaim all warranties, express or implied, including, but not limited to, implied warranties of merchantability and fitness for a particular purpose. The Author and the Publisher do not warrant that defects will be corrected, or that any website or any server that makes this book available is free of viruses or other harmful components. The Author does not warrant or make any representations regarding the use or the results of the use of the materials in this book in terms of their correctness, accuracy, reliability, or otherwise. Applicable law may not allow the exclusion of implied warranties, so the above exclusion may not apply to you.

Under no circumstances, including, but not limited to, negligence, shall the Author or the Publisher be liable for any special or consequential damages that result from the use of, or the inability to use this book, even if the Author, the Publisher, or an authorized representative has been advised of the possibility of such damages. Applicable law may not allow the limitation or exclusion of liability or incidental or consequential damages, so the above limitation or exclusion may not apply to you. In no event shall the Author or Publisher total liability to you for all damages, losses, and causes of action (whether in contract, tort, including but not limited to, negligence or otherwise) exceed the amount paid by you, if any, for this book.

You agree to hold the Author and the Publisher of this book, principals, agents, affiliates, and employees harmless from any and all liability for all claims for damages due to injuries, including attorney fees and costs, incurred by you or caused to third parties by you, arising out of the products, services, and activities discussed in this book, excepting only claims for gross negligence or intentional tort.

You agree that any and all claims for gross negligence or intentional tort shall be settled solely by confidential binding arbitration per the American Arbitration Association's commercial arbitration rules. All arbitration must occur in the municipality where the Author's principal place of business is located. Arbitration fees and costs shall be split equally, and you are solely responsible for your own lawyer fees.

Facts and information are believed to be accurate at the time they were placed in this book. All data provided in this book is to be used for information purposes only. The information contained within is not intended to provide specific legal, financial, tax, physical or mental health advice, or any other advice whatsoever, for any individual or company and should not be relied upon in that regard. The services described are only offered in jurisdictions where they may be legally offered. Information provided is not all-inclusive, and is limited to information that is made available and such information should not be relied upon as all-inclusive or accurate.

For more information about this policy, please contact the Author at the e-mail address listed in the Copyright Notice at the front of this book.

Affiliate Compensation & Material Connections Disclosure

This book may contain hyperlinks to websites and information created and maintained by other individuals and organizations. The Author and the Publisher do not control or guarantee the accuracy, completeness, relevance, or timeliness of any information or privacy policies posted on these linked websites.

You should assume that all references to products and services in this book are made because material connections exist between the Author or Publisher and the providers of the mentioned products and services ("Provider"). You should also assume that all hyperlinks within this book are affiliate links for (a)

122

the Author, (b) the Publisher, or (c) someone else who is an affiliate for the mentioned products and services (individually and collectively, the "Affiliate").

The Affiliate recommends products and services in this book based in part on a good faith belief that the purchase of such products or services will help readers in general.

The Affiliate has this good faith belief because (a) the Affiliate has tried the product or service mentioned prior to recommending it or (b) the Affiliate has researched the reputation of the Provider and has made the decision to recommend the Provider's products or services based on the Provider's history of providing these or other products or services.

The representations made by the Affiliate about products and services reflect the Affiliate's honest opinion based upon the facts known to the Affiliate at the time this book was published.

Because there is a material connection between the Affiliate and Providers of products or services mentioned in this book, you should always assume that the Affiliate may be biased because of the Affiliate's relationship with a Provider and/or because the Affiliate has received or will receive something of value from a Provider.

Perform your own due diligence before purchasing a product or service mentioned in this book.

The type of compensation received by the Affiliate may vary. In some instances, the Affiliate may receive complimentary products (such as a review copy), services, or money from a Provider prior to mentioning the Provider's products or services in this book.

In addition, the Affiliate may receive a monetary commission or non-monetary compensation when you take action by clicking on a hyperlink in this book. This includes, but is not limited to, when you purchase a product or service from a Provider after clicking on an affiliate link in this book.

Purchase Price

Although the Publisher believes the price is fair for the value that you receive, you understand and agree that the purchase price for this book has been arbitrarily set by the Publisher. This price bears no relationship to objective standards.

Due Diligence

You are advised to do your own due diligence when it comes to making any decisions. Use caution and seek the advice of qualified professionals before acting upon the contents of this book or any other information. You shall not consider any examples, documents, or other content in this book or otherwise provided by the Author or Publisher to be the equivalent of professional advice.

The Author and the Publisher assume no responsibility for any losses or damages resulting from your use of any link, information, or opportunity contained in this book or within any other information disclosed by the Author or the Publisher in any form whatsoever.

YOU SHOULD ALWAYS CONDUCT YOUR OWN INVESTIGATION (PERFORM DUE DILIGENCE) BEFORE BUYING PRODUCTS OR SERVICES FROM ANYONE OFFLINE OR VIA THE INTERNET. THIS INCLUDES PRODUCTS AND SERVICES SOLD VIA HYPERLINKS EMBEDDED IN THIS BOOK.

CPSIA information can be obtained at www.ICGtesting.com
Printed in the USA
LVOW10s2004201113

362115LV00025B/1478/P